MW01282090

Journaling

Being Mindful
of World Around You
through Daily Journaling

This journal belongs to:

_____

_____

_____

30 Days of Journaling:
Being Mindful of the World Around you through Daily Journaling
Prompt Journaling Series – Book 2

CONTACT THE AUTHOR

Pam Tremble
Stationery Nerd • 5036 Dixie Highway #300536 • Waterford, MI 48330
books@stationerynerd.com
https://stationeryNERD.com/books

J 30 DAYS OF
Journaling

Being Mindful
of World Around You
through Daily Journaling

PAM TREMBLE

stationeryNERD
.COM

Mindful Journaling

When you think of mindfulness you probably imagine sitting cross-legged on a cushion on the floor, eyes closed, focused on your breathing, and humming a soft om to yourself. It seems that the idea of being mindful has somehow become closely tied to the practice of meditation, yoga or being silent and just breathing.

That stereotypical definition has a place in the overall practice of being mindful and is helpful for a lot of people and there is a place for that type of meditative mindfulness. However, that's not what we're going to be exploring in this book.

Meditation may be about being in the present moment, but you can also use your noticing skills to be mindful of the world around you. You live in an amazing world. But when was the last time you took the time to truly explore that world?

When was the last time you took the time explore all the wonderful aspects of your community and your neighborhood? How often do you stop to pay attention to the way your community celebrates a specific holiday or the different seasons?

How often have you stopped to chat with a neighbor and learned something new about the people who live so close to you? And what about the details of your own home? When was the last time you peeked inside your junk drawer or why you surround yourself with the types of possessions you choose to keep?

In the journaling prompts that follow I'll take you through all those areas of your world. You'll be journaling about your community, your neighborhood, your home, and even yourself and your family. We'll start with the outermost circle of your world and slowly bring the focus inward to your own home.

ANALOG vs. DIGITAL

We spend so much time at the computer these days that it might seem logical to just fire up a word processing document and start typing. If that's you're the only option, then yes… do that. But science tells us that going analog is better. The physical-to-mental connection helps to create a more solid foundation in our mind which allows journaling to have a greater impact on our lives.

In the pages that follow you'll see that I've provided some space for you to write. It's only a tiny bit of space, I know. I encourage you to use a separate blank journal to write your daily entries – pull out one of those half-filled journals and fill it up! The space in this book can be used to jot down your initial thoughts or an outline of what you plan to journal about.

15 MINUTES PER DAY

Journaling doesn't need to take a lot of time each day to be effective. If you only have 5 minutes, that's fine. If you want to spend hours in your journal each day, that's fine too. For this 30-day challenge, I've crafted the daily prompts to take about 15 minutes per day of journaling. Set a timer if you'd like. Or just write until you're finished.

PRIVACY & TRUST

Your journal is a very personal place. A place where your private thoughts are protected from nosy friends or family members. Your journal is a safe place where your raw, honest, and intimate thoughts are put on paper. It's where you can be vulnerable without the fear of judgment or ridicule. If you have family or friends who don't understand the importance of this level of privacy, be sure to have a conversation with them about that expectation of trust. Or find a really good hiding place for your journal!

DAILY PROMPTS

Each day I will provide a new prompt. Something that will guide you in your journaling session and help you get words on the page. I have been strategic with the order of these prompts so they will guide you through an exploration of the world around you.

We'll begin with prompts about the wider world around you including your country, state and region of the world. Then we'll move closer to home and journal about your community then your neighborhood. Finally we'll explore your home - not just your physical house, but also the places that have personal meaning to you and how your life is different because of those places.

Some prompts will be hard and require introspection. Some will be fun and give you a chance to explore your silly side. I hope the prompts I've prepared for you will give help you gain a greater appreciation for the world around you.

Each prompt is more than just a single question. I've given you ideas for how to explore the prompt for fully and in many cases, given you a few different angles to explore with that simple question. However, if the prompt for the day just doesn't speak to you or if you've got something else pressing to write about... by all mean, do what is right for you.

NO RIGHT OR WRONG

One of the biggest lessons I want you to take away from this challenge is that there is no ONE way to journal. There's no right way. There's no wrong way. Journaling is very personal and whatever you write is exactly the right thing to write. And when I say there should be no judgment in journaling... that means YOU too. You're not allowed to scold yourself for "not journaling correctly." Be kind to yourself. Whatever you're doing inside your journal is 100% right.

What's a Stationery Nerd?

I bet you're probably wondering what the heck is a stationery nerd, anyway!

Hi! I'm Pam and I've been obsessed with stationery goodies, back-to-school supplies, office products, paper and notebooks for as long as I can remember. I probably own too many pens, too many notebooks, too many art supplies, and too many ways to store all those things.

I'm also a self-professed nerd. Websters Dictionary defines a nerd as "*a single-minded expert in a particular technical field.*" Yep, that's pretty accurate when it comes to stationery, for me. I'll obsessively research a particular stationery supply before deciding which one to choose (who am I kidding, I never choose just one!).

TEACHING IS MY PASSION

I am passionate about helping people live a better life by teaching techniques in journaling, planning, and playing with stationery... and of course, buying the right supplies for those pursuits.

I'm an analog girl at heart and find that project planning and tracking tasks on paper are most productive for me. I'm happy to teach you my techniques and what works for me – and maybe somewhere along the way you'll discover what works best for you, too. The more ideas we can share together, the more ways we can help each other be more productive.

I AM NOT A PURIST

We can learn from each other by openly sharing our individual methods of journaling and planning. I keep a bullet journal, but my "bujo" looks nothing like the official Bullet Journal Method developed by Ryder Carroll. I created a planning system that fits my life, not Ryder's.

I also write Morning Pages, but my form of morning pages does not follow the exact method set forth by Julia Cameron (*the practice of writing, in longhand, three full pages of stream of consciousness journaling before you do anything else in the morning).* I credit the original system for putting me on the path of daily journaling, but over the years I've developed my own style and set my own rules.

On the Stationery Nerd website, one of the most popular articles is called, "I am not a bullet journal purist." I write about the system of journaling and planning that works for me. But even now, a year or so later, the methods I wrote about then have evolved into what I'm doing today.

What I'm trying to say is that you don't need to follow anyone else's method (mine included!) to be a stationery nerd and live a life that you love. Figure out what works for you and go all-in until you have developed your own definition of nerdiness. You have my full permission to do your own thing!

JOIN THE STATIONERY NERD HERD

Yes, there's a Nerd Herd! You should come join us. Find the group on Facebook and you'll find yourself surrounded by people from all over the world who also love journaling, planning, paper, pens, washi tape, and all the stationery they can amass. Find us at fb.com/groups/StationeryNerdHerd

There are other ways to connect with me, too. Flip to the end of this book for a list of social media channels where you can find Stationery Nerd online.

LET'S START JOURNALING!

Ready to start journaling? Let's go! I'd love to hear how you're doing along the way. Don't hesitate to reach out if you're struggling or have questions. I'm here for you! Let's do this together!

Day 1

Using your five senses - sight, smell, hearing, taste, touch - journal about your immediate surroundings.

Take a moment to sit quietly before you begin journaling. In turn, tune into each of your five senses and observe the information that each is collecting about the world around you.

SMELL: This is one of the most powerful of all the senses (or so says science). A specific scent can bring back memories, influence your mood and even affect your work performance. What are the scents in your space today?

HEARING: Close your eyes and just listen. Is it quiet or noisy? Is there birdsong or the mechanical hum from appliances or a breeze rustling the curtains at the window?

SIGHT: Look around and observe what you see. Are you in a familiar place? Is there anything new in the space that you didn't notice before. What color seems to dominate the area? Do you see loved ones nearby or strangers?

TASTE: Have you ever had to describe the taste of something that you've eaten a hundred times in your life? The flavor is so familiar to you that you just take for granted that everyone else knows it too. But our taste buds aren't limited to just tasting a type of food. My grandfather used to say he could "taste the rain" when a storm was brewing.

TOUCH: What are you holding right now? Since this is a journaling exercise, it is likely a pen and a journal. How does it feel in your hand? Are there ridges or is it smooth? Does the feel of it change if you close your eyes? What else is within arms reach that you can touch right now? The fabric of your clothes or the surface of a desk?

Day 2

What is your town, state or country known for?

What is the name of the city where you live? Where is it located in the world? What's the climate like? Is it rural or urban? Are the people who live in your city laid back and relaxed or is there always a sense of hustle and bustle?

Is there a landmark or specific attraction in the area that tourists visit? Describe the last time you visited the areas of your city where a tourist might visit but locals don't go as often. For instance, if you live in New York City, is the Statue of Liberty just a part of the landscape in your everyday life or does it still stand as an awe-inspiring landmark, as it would for a visitor who is seeing it for the first time?

Think about the larger region where you live. Is your state or country known for something specific? Do you live in a farming community where a specific crop grows especially well? Is there an industry that defines your region?

For instance, I live on the outskirts of a small city in Michigan. My neighborhood is surrounded by farmland but here in Michigan, we are known for the automotive industry since the headquarters for Ford, Chrysler, General Motors are located in the Detroit metro area. If I lived in northern Michigan, my town might be known for cherry crops or ski resorts.

Have you ever been "a tourist in your own town?" What do you love most about where you live? As you complete your journaling entry for today, are you inspired to visit something new in your town?

Day 3

Write about a nearby body of water.

Do you live near some type of body of water? An ocean, lake, pond, river, stream, or creek? Or maybe it's a marsh or wetlands.... or just a big mud puddle.

Is your city or state defined by that body of water? Maybe you live on the ocean coastline where beautiful beaches are the primary tourist attraction for your area. Or maybe you live in a rural setting where the closest body of water is a creek that runs along the back of your property.

It doesn't matter how big and grand or small and humble it is, let's just focus on that for today.

Are there activities that revolve around that body of water? Do you visit often? What activities in your city or state encourage people to gather at the water's edge. Are there festivals? Maybe boat races or swimming demonstrations. Or maybe the best thing about that mud puddle down the street is putting on your rubber boots and playing in the rain. Did you jump in mud puddles when you were a kid (I love my childhood memories of that!)?

Take some time today to journal about how the water makes you feel. Do you have feelings of excitement, playfulness, and adventure when you think of going to the water for the day? Or is the water's edge a place of relaxation, calm, and solitude for you? How often do you get to go and what's a day look like when you head for the water?

Day 4

What art is in your life?

As an artist, I love the idea of having a full day dedicated to exploring my city to find as many artistic attractions as I can see in a day. Do you notice the art in your world, too?

Does your town have a local museum or art gallery? Maybe it's an outdoor art installation or statue garden that attracts widespread attention in the region. Is there a summertime art show or street festival that celebrates art where hundreds of artisans line the streets to sell their works of art? What are those experiences like? Journal about a recent visit to one of those attractions.

Are there specific colors or styles of art that attract your attention more than others? Is there a local artist that you admire? Or one of the great masters of art history whose art is reproduced on posters or prints in your home (or even on the cover of a notebook or journal)?

Do you have art hanging in your home or at your office or workplace? Or maybe you're still in school and taking an art class (or just doodle all over your math homework). Describe the art that hangs in your home. Journal about the art that you create. Do you share your love of art with anyone else in your family or friend circle?

Day 5

What is your relationship with emergency personnel or first responders in your community?

In your community, there are dozens (or hundreds) of men and women who serve, protect, and help their fellow citizens. They are dedicated to the well-being, safety, and rescue of those they serve. Police forces, firefighters, emergency medical teams, and rescue crews. In addition, we have the armed forces – Army, Navy, Coast Guard, Marines – or whatever the branches of the military are named in your country.

I find that we rarely think about what other people do for their jobs until we have some type of encounter with them that affects our own personal life. Have you ever had an instance where a first responder came to your aid? Do you know of anyone in your family or friend circle whose life was saved because of the quick response and dedication of those who protect your community?

Have you had a negative encounter (like a speeding ticket or car accident) that sticks in your mind? How were you treated? What did you feel? Were your emotions out of control or on-edge? How did the situation get resolved?

Take some time today to journal about the emergency personnel in your community and how they've touched your life. Is there something you can do to support them and show them that you appreciate the work they do?

Day 6

How are you involved in your community?

There are many ways to get involved in your community that give you an opportunity to help others in need or shape the policy and direction of your town. Think about all the ways that you are involved. Do you volunteer for a local charitable organization? Are you active with your church or synagogue by attending services or extending your service to those in need?

There are other ways to be involved, too. Politics, committees, and boards all need worthy citizens to help govern the bodies they lead. Have you ever run for public office? What was it and what were your responsibilities? What committees have you served on and what projects did you help organize? Maybe you're a member of a board of directors in your town – describe that experience and what it means to serve in that capacity.

Or maybe you're the person who gathers people together and organizes groups who do good deeds for your community. Have you ever organized a clean-up day in your town? Gathering a group of friends together, armed with trash bags and tools to help clean up a park, beach or other public space is a great way to serve others in your community.

Journal about how you've been involved in your community and what it means to you.

Day 7

How do you get your news?

It used to be that there were only a couple of ways to hear the latest news about your town. Either you read about it in the local newspaper or you tuned into the local news channel on television. In fact, I remember when the only time news was broadcast on TV was for the morning news show, at noon and 6:00 p.m. and once again at 11:00 p.m. If you missed one of those broadcasts, you'd have to wait for the next one. There wasn't a website you could visit to catch up on the stories you missed. And that local newspaper? It was only published once a week.

But now we are in the technological age of information where news is available around the clock on at least 743 different news channels or websites (probably more, actually). Newspapers are becoming a thing of the past and many have stopped running physical papers completely – publishing instead a digital version on the web only.

CNN and Fox run news 24/7 with buildings full of reporters, news anchors, and special investigative teams creating long-form news content. There are daily podcasts and YouTube news channels. And don't forget that all this news is now global and doesn't just focus on the country where you live.

From which news outlets do you get your news? Local broadcast news? National or international news? Do you rely exclusively on Internet news channels or social media chatter? Or maybe you don't care about all the news of the world and prefer instead to just walk down the street and get the neighborhood gossip at the local coffee shop.

Day 8

What type of shopping is available near you?

Do you live in an area where shopping is a favorite pastime and there are a dozen stores lining Main Street? Or maybe you live in a rural area where the closest store is an hour away and that store only sells feed for farm animals and tractor repair supplies. Are there "big box" stores (Walmart, Kohl's, Target) that dominate the shopping landscape? Do you have malls bustling with people? Or maybe your town is known for a tourist area where elite shopping boutiques are open seasonally to serve the people who visit your area.

Take some time to think about what types of shopping centers are available to you and which ones you visit most often. Where do you buy groceries? Clothes? Household supplies or home improvement materials? Are there specialty stores where you'd likely go when you need to buy a gift for a loved one?

And speaking of shopping – are you an avid shopper? Or do you avoid stores like the plague and prefer shopping online instead? Today's journal entry is a great opportunity to list all your favorite stores and why you love them so much.

Day 9

What are the antiquing and thrifting opportunities in your area?

For those who are passionate antique collectors, you'll know every possible antique shop within a 100-mile radius. The same goes for thrifters and bargain hunters. Or maybe you're one who loves a great garage sale to find hidden treasures and have a weekly routine of bargain hunting in your neighborhood.

First take some time to journal about the type of things you like to find at antique shops, thrift shops, flea markets or garage sales. Are you an equal opportunity bargain hunter or do you have your eye on one particular type of treasure?

I have a friend who loves finding vintage clothing and turning it into the latest fashion statement in her wardrobe. I personally love hunting for vintage stationery, used notebooks (usually with a treasure trove of scribblings from someone who lived many years ago), and old office supplies.

How often do you shop at these types of stores? Do you have a regular schedule or do you go shopping only on special trips with a group of like-minded friends? Maybe you make a day of it and stop for lunch midway through the day to refuel for more shopping.

Describe some of the treasures you've found and what they mean to you. How do you display them in your home or use them in your daily life?

Day 10

What type of theater or stage production opportunities are in your community?

If you live in New York City, Chicago, London, Toronto, or Tokyo you're used to having access to plays, musicals, or other award-winning productions. But the big stage isn't the only place to see outstanding performances. Community theater groups, high school drama clubs, and even local churches that produce holiday performances are all great options for enjoying plays and musicals.

Or maybe your only experience so far is the Thanksgiving Day performance at your son's daycare where he played the pilgrim or your daughter's dance recital. Or perhaps Shakespeare in the Park?

When did you last attend an event like this? What was it and who did you go with? Describe the performance and how the plot unfolded throughout the show. Do you recall the actor's names and anything about their biography from the program pamphlet? How did the performance go? Did you notice any mistakes or flubbing of lines? Were you swept up in the story and feel all the emotions of the actors on stage?

How often do you attend productions like this? Do you wish you could go more often? Take a few minutes to search the schedules for your local theater locations to see which performances catch your attention. Did you buy tickets?

Day 11

Describe the nightlife in your community.

When was the last time you went out with a group of friends and let loose at a nightclub? Alright, maybe that's not the type of nightlife you prefer, but thankfully there are lots of different ways to define "nightlife."

According to Wikipedia, nightlife is:

> ...a collective term for entertainment that is popular from the late evening into the early hours of the morning. It includes pubs, bars, nightclubs, parties, live music, concerts, and shows.

Are you the type of person who fits into the definition above? Do you love going out with friends to stay out until the break of dawn? Describe your experience and why you love it so much (or why you don't love it, if that applies).

However, for our journaling exercise today, let's expand that definition. Nightlife could simply mean going on a date with your spouse, away from the kids for a few hours. Do you hire a babysitter so you can have a date night on a regular basis? Or maybe nightlife means going for a moonlit stroll to enjoy the quiet of the evening after the sun goes down.

And then there's a vast array of us (me included) who think nightlife means changing into pajamas early, making a bowl of popcorn and curling up with your sweetie on the couch to watch a movie.

Describe what a fun night might look like for you.

Day 12

What festivals, fairs or celebrations happen in your town?

Does your community have a signature event that it is well known for? Maybe it's a big festival that shuts down most of the town and the festivities take over to celebrate for a weekend (or longer). Is there a carnival or fair the comes to town every summer? Or maybe your town goes all-out to celebrate a specific holiday.

Here in Michigan there's a festival in every town across the state. We have everything from the 10-day *Cherry Festival* in Traverse City, a weekend barbecue cook-off call *Pig Gig* in Bay City, and the week of *Cheeseburger In Paradise* in Caseville. Or maybe the *Fish Sandwich Festival*, *Potato Festival*... wait, why are all these festivals about food? We have more that aren't food-related – like the *Folk Music Festival* and the *River Roar* boat races in the next town over. Needless to say, we have a lot of festivals around the area.

I'm sure your part of the world is no different. Do you enjoy attending these types of events when they take over the town? Which one is your favorite? Or maybe the question I should ask is which one do your friends drag you to and force you to have a good time?

Take some time to journal about the last festival you attended, what the theme was, who you went with and what you did while you were there. Are there other celebrations coming in the near future that you plan to attend?

Day 13

What holiday is happening right now?

No matter what time of the year it is right now, there's likely to be a holiday just around the corner (or just past).

Are you planning anything special for this holiday? Do you celebrate or does your family have a special tradition? What does your community do to honor the upcoming holiday? Are there festivals, street fairs, or special concerts scheduled?

As I'm writing this question we are preparing for Thanksgiving. Not only does my family plan a big celebration with a special meal of turkey, stuffing, mashed potatoes, pumpkin pie and all the other trimmings of a traditional Thanksgiving dinner. But we also have several traditions surrounding this day. My dad goes all-out in decorating the yard for Christmas and in recent years, it's become tradition that after dinner we all trek outside to stand across the street as he turns the lights on for the first time.

A local city near me hosts the Turkey Trot, which is road race for runners and walkers held on Thanksgiving morning (this year there will be about 16,000 in the "flock"). And you can't forget the Thanksgiving Day parades, football games, shopping crowds, and post-dinner naps.

Which holiday is coming up for you? Take some time to journal about what that holiday means to you and how you celebrate with your family, friends, or your community.

Day 14

What season of the year is it right now and what's happening around you?

Do you live in a part of the world where seasons are clearly defined and nature changes dramatically as one season transitions into another? Is summer vastly different than winter? Is the way nature evolves different in spring and fall? Or do you live in a place where it stays pretty much the same year-round?

I love to think about how vastly different seasons are in the Northern Hemisphere compared to the Southern Hemisphere. When North America is celebrating winter with snowy conditions with layers of winter hats, scarves and mittens and building snowmen in the yard...our friends in Australia are experiencing winter with sweltering hot days of sunshine and backyard picnics. And those who live closer to the equator have seasons that don't change in such a dramatic way.

With each change of season, we also have changes in our personal lives. Do you put away the clothes of one season and unpack different clothes from storage for the next season? Packing away beach clothes in favor of unpacking sweaters and jackets. Maybe you change the decor`in your house? Does your neighborhood change, too? Do you decorate your yard for the different seasons?

Take some time to journal about what happens to the natural environment during season changes and what it's like right now, during this time of the year. Also explore some of the ways that you, personally change as the seasons change.

Day 15

What is the natural environment like in your world?

Do you live in the city or in the country? Do you have lots of green space or is it mostly concrete and steel? Are you surrounded by trees, grass, flowers, and animals or are you surrounded by skyscrapers, honking cars, and pedestrians? Or maybe your natural environment is a mix of both city and country where you have access to both of scenes.

Are you the type of person who loves to get outside and explore nature? Hiking or biking on trails to absorb the aroma of nature can be a peaceful experience for some (or it could be stress-inducing for others). How often are you able to experience a natural environment?

If you live in a busy city environment, do you seek out nature from time to time? Maybe you bring plants into your house to add some lively color or maybe you escape the city on the weekend and drive to your favorite park or nearby town.

Take some time to write about what you see around you in the nature. Look out the window, what do you see. Are there trees? Do you hear birds singing? What color are the flowers or shrubs outside your window? How does this make you feel? How important is nature to you and how often do you notice it?

Day 16

What is your primary mode of transportation?

Have you ever thought about all the ways that people around the world get from one place to another? If you drive a car as your primary mode of transportation, have you ever given thought to those who don't own a car but instead get around on a bike or walk everywhere? Different parts of the world have different ways of getting from one place to another that depends on the environment in which they live, how far they have to travel, and the types of transportation options they have available.

What is your mode of transportation? Where do you typically go with that vehicle? Do you choose a different transport method for different areas of your life? For instance, do you use a car to get to your job, but if you need to make a trip to the corner store, it's easier to hop on your bike for the errand? Or maybe it's difficult to own a car in your area and it's easier to use public transit like a bus, subway or train.

Maybe you don't have far to go and you prefer walking. Do you have a skateboard or electric scooter? Do you use it as transportation or is that just for fun and play?

Take some time today and journal about how you typically get around in your world. What are all the ways that you could get from one place to another? Do you have some vehicles that are more for fun than serious transit? Do you have any strong feelings about one type of transportation over another? When you're out of town, do you take your vehicle with you or do you rely on the options of that new place?

Day 17

What is your job like?

What type of job do you have? A job might be one where you perform work for someone else and they give you a paycheck in exchange or a job might be any type of responsibility you have that is assigned to you. For instance, the job of being a parent is a huge responsibility and requires a lot of work. Or the job of being a volunteer also comes with plenty of work to keep the mission of that organization moving forward.

How do you define the word "job" and what does it mean to you? Describe the job you have and if it's a traditional job (with a paycheck) or something that isn't always referred to with that term. We all have a lot of different jobs in life, so there might not be just a single answer for this question. Today we'll explore what your job is like and what it means to you. You can either journal about all the different jobs you hold or pick just one or two for today's journaling.

What's the environment of your job? What's the culture? Are there people you work with that you don't enjoy being around or do you love the people you work with? Do you have a career path or promotion plan? How are you getting better at your job each day? Do you enjoy it or do you dread each day? What's your job title and how long have you worked there?

Who do you work with? Do you have a boss, coworkers, colleagues or customers? How often do you perform the work? How much are you paid .... Or what type of "currency" are you paid with? For instance, if you have a traditional job, you're paid in money, but if your job is a stay at home mom, you'll be paid in hugs and kisses.

Day 18

Trash. Recycling. Composting. How does that work in your city?

Have you ever thought about how trash, recycling, and composting work in another city or country? Unless you have an interest in environmental issues or work in the waste management industry, you probably haven't given it a second thought. The routine that you have set for your trash is just that... routine. And quite often, when something is a routine, it's not something we think about on a regular basis.

Take some time to write down your routine as it relates to trash, recycling, and composting of yard waste and food scraps. Do you have curbside pickup of these items? Do you have to take your recycling to a facility for processing? Do you have a compost bin in the backyard where you turn your yard waste and food scraps into beautiful rich new soil? Are you passionate about protecting the environment by recycling as many items as you can?

Several years ago I was the Recycling Education Manager for my local government agency. Part of my job was to teach 3rd and 4th grade students about recycling and composting. I helped classrooms begin their own composting bin and teach about how worms eat their trash. I would lead students in art projects where we would turn junk mail or scraps of paper into a new sheet of paper. You never realize how much there is to learn about recycling until you have to teach it to a roomful of eager 3rd graders.

Is there anything about your community's trash, recycling and composting service that you'd like to change? Is there a way you can get more involved in environmental conservation efforts in your neighborhood?

Day 19

Who are your neighbors?

Do you live in a neighborhood where everyone knows each other and gets along like a second family? Maybe you hold a summer block party with barbecue grills, dishes to pass, and organized kids games. Or maybe your neighbors all compete for the most beautifully decorated house for the holidays. Are there regular dinner parties with friends down the street? Do you know everyone's name, the names of all the kids?

I wonder how common it is to live in a community where your neighbors feel like an extension of your family. Or if most people are like me and can't remember my neighbors' names but I wave at them when we're both outside at the same time. I'll stop and chat for a few minutes if there's something to chat about. And I know for sure at one point I knew their names even if I forgot what they are now.

Maybe you have one or two special friends in your neighborhood but you don't necessarily know everyone all along the entire street. How did you become friends? What types of activities do you do together? Do you go to each others' homes or do you prefer to go out to a restaurant or another location instead?

Do you have a neighborhood association or some type of committee who makes decisions on behalf of the entire area? Do you pay dues or an association fee? What types of services are provided?

Take some time to write about your neighborhood. What do you like most about where you live? What's the general feeling, the culture, or atmosphere that defines the community? Do you wish there was something different about your neighborhood?

Day 20

What is your home like?

There are dozens of different kinds of homes. What is yours like? Not only can you explore the physical place in which you live, but you can also journal about how that home feels and what it means to you. Everyone has a different definition of home, too. The place where you live might not feel like home to you. In fact, you might consider home to be the place where you grew up and going back home has a whole different meaning to you.

What is your house like? Is it an actual house or something else? Apartment, condo, duplex or multi-family dwelling? Cabin in the woods? Hut on the beach? Tent, camper, van or RV that travels wherever you want to go? How many bedrooms and bathrooms do you have? How big or small is it? What is your decorating style? Does it have curb-appeal with elaborate landscaping? Do you have a garden or flower bed?

Who else lives with you? Are you on your own with a pet or two or is your house filled with lots of family and friends? Do you have roommates? How often do you have guests who sleep in the guest bedroom (or on the sofa)? Or maybe you're the one who lives with someone else in their home.

What comforts do you have around you? What is your favorite room and why do you love it so much? What does it mean to you to have a place that you call home?

Day 21

Where you get your fresh produce?

It's time to fix dinner and you're craving a big green salad with all the fixings. You open the refrigerator and pull out everything you'll need – lettuce, carrots, peppers, radishes, tomatoes and more. Where did all those yummy veggies come from? And what about fruit and herbs and other seasonal foods that are grown or raised locally?

Do you have a garden where you grow your own fruits and vegetables? Maybe you have a window garden for herbs or a small kitchen garden just outside the back door of your house. If you don't have a garden, maybe the local farmer's market is your go-to place for fresh produce.

What is available in your area and how often do you frequent these locally grown shopping options rather than a traditional grocery store? At my local big-box grocery store, I can get any type of fruit or vegetable I want from anywhere in the world, any time of the year. Sometimes the prices reflect the fact that the growing season has ended and that item needed to be flown in from a faraway land. But whenever possible, I prefer to buy my produce from a local farmer.

Take some time today to journal about what types of fresh produce are available in your area. If you keep your own garden, describe the types of plants you have and how your family enjoys the harvest. Are you one of those gardeners who accidentally planted too much zucchini and now you're known as the zucchini-gifter wherever you go?

What's your favorite vegetable and fruit? How do you get it and how do you fix it when it's time to make something for dinner?

Day 22

What do you grow inside your house?

Originally, I thought this type of question would apply to things like house plants or window herb gardens. But then I started thinking about all the other things that grow inside a house.

Grow – /grō/
verb

- Undergo natural development by increasing in physical size or progress to maturity
- Gradually come to feel or know something over time. To improve or become better.

Write down a list of as many different kinds of things that can grow in your house. You can start with house plant, window herb gardens, or even indoor fruits and veggies.

But what else grows? Children. Waistlines. Love. Faith. Impatience. Intellect. And that "science experiment" that lurks at the back of your refrigerator. Can you think of other types of things that grow?

Once you have a list, pick one or two off that list and spend some time journaling about what growth means to you. Are you a talented gardener who can make any house plant flourish under your care? Do you have a brood of children who are growing so quickly that you can't keep up with their ever-changing shoe sizes?

What does it mean to tend to and nurture the living things inside your house?

Day 23

What's in your fridge?

Are you the type of person who keeps everything neat and orderly in your refrigerator? Every shelf has a specific assignment and all the bowls and jars and jugs are lined up in perfect rows. All the condiments are well within their "best by" date and somewhere in a journal, there lurks a complete inventory of the contents of your refrigerator. Or is that just an imaginary refrigerator in an appliance catalog with a staged family?

More likely you fall into one of two other categories:

1. The fridge is bare and you don't really use the refrigerator except when you bring home leftovers from the restaurant, or

2. The fridge is a free-for-all and you're not entirely sure there isn't a small family of monsters lurking in the crisper drawer.

Without looking, could you write down the contents of your refrigerator? Take some time today to write about groceries. (I know, strange journaling topic, but stick with me...) When was the last time you were at the grocery store?

What type of grocery shopper are you? Do you go in with a list and only buy what's planned or do you wing it and usually forget something. Do you go to the store often or only once or twice a month? Do you like to keep plenty of food in the fridge, freezer, or pantry so you've always got choices at dinnertime?

How do you think your food shopping habits are different than those of your parents or grandparents? What will your great-grandchildren think about the way you shop for or prepare food.

Day 24

What's in your junk drawer?

I know this is a scary journaling prompt. But don't worry, we'll get through it together. We all have a junk drawer – that one place in the house where all the miscellaneous bits and pieces of junk lives. It's not always junk, of course. Sometimes it's just stuff that should be put away somewhere else in the house. And it might not be an actual drawer. Mine is a basket that I have on a shelf on a bookcase in the living room.

Similar to the journaling exercise we had yesterday, can you write a list of all the things in that drawer without looking? What does your junk drawer look like – or if it's not a drawer, what is it? Is it a jumbled mess or do you have it compartmentalized with tidy drawer dividers? Are there important things stored here? What are they?

Once you've written a list from memory, go take a peek inside your drawer. Rifle around a bit. Pick one thing and take it back to your journaling space. Take some time to journal about the item you chose from the drawer. What is it? Describe it as if you need to explain it to someone who has never seen one before. Color. Shape. Size. What is it made of? What's it used for? Why is it in your junk drawer instead of somewhere else in your home?

And now I'm curious, did this prompt cause you to clean your junk drawer?

Day 25

What do you look forward to most when you return home?

Have you ever been on a long vacation or extended business trip and at the end of an exhausting week you just want to be home and in your own space again?

Is there something specific about home that you long for when you're gone? Maybe it's sleeping in your own bed. Or having a closet and dresser instead of living out of a suitcase. Do you have creature comforts that you miss when you're away? It might be that you are one who thrives on routine and can't wait to get back to a normal schedule again.

I tend to be a homebody and have created a cozy atmosphere for myself with a few different nooks in my house where I can retreat for some quiet time. I have a reading nook in my bedroom and a cozy sofa with lots of pillows in the living room for Netflix marathons.

Have you every heard of "post-vacation depression?" Psychologists suggest that the best way to avoid getting the blues after you return from vacation is journaling. Specifically to record the small, happy memories of your vacation as soon as you return home. Imagine that! Journaling to the rescue again.

Take some time today to journal about what you love about being at home after an extended time away.

Day 26

Do you have animals in your life?

Are you one of the 38% of households that has at least one dog as a pet? Or the 25% of homes with a cat? Or maybe your pet is a bird, reptile or rodent (or a pet rock). As a pet owner you know how special our animals are and how they become a true part of the family.

What does it mean to you to be a pet owner. Do you have a sense of obligation or responsibility for your pets that you weren't expecting before you became a pet owner? What is life like at your home with your pets?

Describe your pet's personality. How did you come up with a name for your pet? Does it live up to its name in any way? What habits does your pet have that are annoying? Loving? Funny? What is your favorite memory of a pet from your childhood or another time in your life? Who do you think benefits more from pet ownership – you or your pet?

Maybe you don't have any pets of your own. Are there other animals in your life? Maybe a dog or cat of a relative or friend that you enjoy the company of? Do you have a bird feeder in the yard? Do visit the ducks at the local park? Or maybe you love visiting the zoo to learn about exotic animals that can't be kept as pets.

Take some time to journal about all the different animals in your life and what it means to you to have a furry friend.

Day 27

What role does technology play in your life?

We are surrounded by technology. In fact, we're so inundated with the constant connection that there's a whole movement around unplugging and going on digital detox diets.

Can you believe that the first cell phone was sold in 1983? (Seems like yesterday, huh?) It was about the size of a loaf of bread and had a whopping 30 minutes of talk time per battery charge. Plus it cost $4,000! Oh my, how times have changed!

Take some time to journal about what role technology plays in your life today and how that has evolved over time. What was your earliest experience with some form of technology? Did you learn to type on a computer or were you taught (like me) on an old manual typewriter? Did you have a rotary phone when you were a kid or have you only ever known mobile phones?

What is one piece of technology that you couldn't live without? And which piece of tech would you love to never have to use again? What other forms of technology has touched your life?

The latest developments in tech is call the "Internet of things," which basically means that everyday objects are not fully connected to the Internet in some way. Our refrigerators tell us when to buy milk. Our door bells tell us who is at the door, even when we're not at home. We can feed our dogs a treat from a remote location. Our cars drive themselves.

How has your life changed over the past 10 years when it comes to technology? How do you think it will change in the next 10 years? Do you want to make any changes to the way you interact with technology that will shape the way your future looks?

Day 28

What do you do for exercise?

Staying active is such an important part of being healthy. We know that science tells us that regular activity helps with physical health as well as emotional well-being. I find that when I get up first thing in the morning and do some type of exercise – even if it's just an hour of housework or running errands – that I feel better for the rest of the day.

What type of exercise do you participate in? Is it a big part of your daily life? Do you have a gym membership? What type of exercise equipment do you have at home? What are your favorite activities?

Or maybe you have an active lifestyle so exercise is just part of your normal daily routine. I once learned a statistic that the number of calories you burn while walking a 5k race (3.1 miles) is about equal to the number of calories you burn doing an hour of vigorous housework or pulling weeds in the garden. (Once I learned that fun fact, I started taking housework more seriously.)

What are your goals for exercising? Do you track your exercise routines in a journal or with an app on your phone? Do you have a work out buddy? Are you physically active so you can stay fit or are you on a weight loss regimen?

Is there any organized exercise programs in your community that you've considered joining? For instance, when I was training for a half-marathon, I joined a training program where I was paired with others at my same pace so we could workout together every week as we prepared for the big race.

Day 29

What is your journaling space like?

As you have worked through these past 28 daily prompts, have you established a specific location for your journaling? Do you have a desk or table that you've set up as your writing space? Do you feel especially creative in this space?

Where is the space located? Are you away from the activity of the house in a quiet corner or separate room? Or do you prefer to be surrounded by the chaos of the household and sitting in the middle of it all? Do you schedule your journaling at the same time every day or do you grab a few moments whenever you can fit it into the day?

Or maybe your journaling space isn't in your home but rather you prefer a mobile journaling experience? Do you visit the bookstore, coffee shop, or library for your journaling time? Or maybe you take your journal to your job with you and carve out some writing time during your lunch break?

Describe the area you're sitting in right now. What is around you? Where are you located and is this your normal place for journaling? Is it quiet or noisy? Is there music playing? Do you have a lot of activity around you or is it a calm environment? Are there other people in the space with you? What is the decor` like? Do you have a cup of tea or coffee? Or a bowl of snacks?

If you don't have a dedicated journaling space, use this prompt as an excuse to fantasize about the perfect space. Would you create a writing retreat? A hideaway for creating a creative environment? Describe what your ideal journaling desk would include. Go ahead, dream big!

Day 30

Where do you buy your journaling supplies?

A Stationery Nerd book wouldn't be complete without a journaling prompt about stationery, right? Where in your world do you buy journaling supplies? Do you have a favorite shop or big-box store in your community where you buy journals, pens, and decorative stickers for your journal? Or maybe you have several stores that you love.

Make a list of the stationery shopping options you have in your local community. How often do you visit each of them? Do they all sell the same types of supplies or is there one that specializes in something different than the others? How often do you visit these shops? How far away are they? Do the cashiers know you by name?

If you don't have any local stationery shops, make a list of your favorite small online shops. Do you visit Etsy or another small business with a line of specialty products? Or do you prefer the big retailers like Amazon or Aliexpress for your stationery needs?

Do you have any stationery shopping buddies who love these types of shops as much as you do?

Think about the last time you went shopping for stationery supplies at one of these stores. Describe your experience. How do you feel when you're inside a stationery shop? Which section do you visit first? What items did you buy during your last visit and which items went on a wish list instead?

Day 31 - bonus prompt!

What have you discovered about the world around you and do you have a greater appreciate for your community?

In the previous 30 days, you've been journaling about the part of the world you live in. Then we brought it a bit closer to home to explore your state, region, and community. And finally, we took a closer look at the things at home including your neighborhood and your own house as well as your personal habits.

My goal with these prompts was to help you explore areas of your world that you might overlook in the daily hustle and bustle of life. Have there been any eye-opening experiences or discoveries that you hadn't thought about before? Is there anything you've journaled about in the past month that you would like to go back and explore further?

And finally, I'm curious if you've been motivated through your journaling to actually get out and explore your community more than you have before. Have you visited an attraction that you wouldn't normally visit? Have you gone to a local theater group's performance? Have you gone out of your way to meet your neighbors? Maybe it's time to go exploring!

Conclusion

I'd love to hear from you and what you've learned from these past 30 days of journaling. You can send an email to me at books@stationerynerd.com or if you're a traditional stationery nerd, feel free to drop me a note in the mail at:

Stationery Nerd
5036 Dixie Highway #300536
Waterford, MI 48330

IDEAS ARE ALWAYS WELCOME

If you've got an idea for new *30 Days of Journaling* topics, I'd love to hear them. This is just the first of many new journaling prompt books to come. So if you have any special requests, drop me a note!

STAY IN TOUCH

Do you love stationery as much as I do? Are you always on the lookout for new stationery discoveries or new ways to use the supplies you have. Come join the Stationery Nerd community!

🌐 Stationerynerd.com/books

📘 fb.com/stationerynerd

📷 instagram.com/stationerynerd.blog

📌 pinterest.com/stationerynerd

▶ youtube.com/stationerynerd

Notes & Journaling Ideas